Lion
& Tiger

ROD THEODOROU

AND

CAROLE TELFORD

First published in Great Britain by Heinemann Library
Halley Court, Jordan Hill, Oxford OX2 8EJ
a division of Reed Educational & Professional Publishing Ltd

MELBOURNE AUCKLAND
FLORENCE PRAGUE MADRID ATHENS
SINGAPORE TOKYO CHICAGO SAO PAULO
PORTSMOUTH NH MEXICO
IBADAN GABORONE JOHANNESBURG
KAMPALA NAIROBI

Designed by Susan Clarke
Cover design by Simon Balley
Illustrations by Adam Abel
Printed in Great Britain by Bath Press Colourbooks, Glasgow

00 99 98 97 96
10 9 8 7 6 5 4 3 2 1

ISBN 0 431 06364 8

British Library Cataloguing in Publication Data
Theodorou, Rod
    Lion & tiger. – (Spot the difference)
    1. Lions – Juvenile literature 2. Tigers – Juvenile literature
    I. Title II. Telford, Carole
    599.7'4428

Acknowledgements
The Publishers would like to thank the following for permission to reproduce photographs:
Mandal Ranjit/FLPA p7; T. Whittaker/FLPA p8; Arthus Bertrand/Ardea London Ltd. p9; Frank
Sneidermeyer/OSF p4; Bob Bennet/OSF p5; Purdy & Matthews/ Survival Anglia pp6, 10,
Planet Earth p22; Gerard Lacz/NHPA pp11, 21; Jonathan Scott/Planet Earth Pictures p12 *top*;
Stephen Krasemann/NHPA p12 *bottom*; Anup Shah/Planet Earth Pictures p13; Ferrero,
Labat/Ardea London Ltd pp3, 17, 20 *top*, 23; P. Perry/FLPA p14; E & D Hosking/FLPA p15
bottom; Charles McDougal/Ardea London Ltd p15 *top*; Roger Tidman/NHPA p16; Clem
Haagner/Ardea Photographics p18; Ralph & Daphne Keller/NHPA p19 *top*; Ardea London
Ltd p19 *bottom*; W Wisniewski/ FLPA p20 *bottom*

Cover photograph reproduced with permission of Norbert Rosing/Oxford Scientific Films,
top; John Downer/Planet Earth Pictures, *bottom*

Every effort has been made to contact copyright holders of any material reproduced in this
book. Any omissions will be rectified in subsequent printings if notice is given to the Publisher.

Contents

Introduction

The cats we keep as pets are close **relations** of the big wild cats. All cats behave in very similar ways. They are almost all carnivores – they only eat meat. They are all fast, expert hunters. Cats have short, powerful jaws and long teeth for tearing meat. They also have sharp claws, to get a good grip on their **prey**.

A male lion

It's amazing!

Although lions are often called 'king of the beasts', they will usually run away from angry rhinos or elephants.

Lions and tigers are the biggest members of the cat family. The male lion has a huge mane of hair around its neck. This protects its neck in fights and makes it look even bigger and stronger. Tigers are the biggest and strongest of all the cats. While lions work together as a team to hunt their prey, tigers hunt alone.

A Siberian tiger – the largest of the five different kinds of tiger.

Where they live

Lions live in the dry grasslands of Africa. The weather there has only two **seasons**: wet and dry. In the wet season there are lots of large animals for lions to hunt. In the dry season many of these animals **migrate**, sometimes even hundreds of miles, to look for water. Lions have to hunt smaller animals; sometimes they even starve.

Although their cubs may be killed by other animals, adult lions have no real enemies in the wild – except humans. Hunting of lions has been stopped in many areas, but people are taking over the grasslands to farm them, pushing the lions out of their territories.

Where lions and tigers live today. A few lions still survive in a reserve in northwest India. ▶

A lioness watches a herd of zebra.

Where tigers live
Where lions live

Tigers live in the hot jungles of Asia, the dry forests and grasslands of India, and the cold, rocky mountains of Siberia. Each kind of tiger has a slightly different coat. The Siberian tiger needs a thicker coat than the others, to keep it warm.

Tigers, like lions, have been hunted and pushed out of their **habitats** by people. Tigers are now an **endangered species**. Soon, some types of tiger may be gone forever.

It's amazing!

Although the Indian tiger is the most common of all tigers, there are only about 3000 of them left in the whole world.

An Indian tiger in its rainforest habitat.

Teeth, claws and paws

Lions and tigers have 30 teeth, designed to help them catch, kill and eat their prey. They have four long canine teeth to stab and hold their prey. They have incisor teeth at the front that are small but sharp enough to break through the tough skin of a buffalo or zebra. Their back molar teeth are as sharp as scissors to slice through meat. The whole jaw is short and powerful. Lions and tigers can bite through bones!

A tiger's teeth

canine

molar

incisor

Lions and tigers have deadly curved claws. Most of the time these are pulled back (retracted) into the paw. This keeps them safe and sharp. Retracted claws make no noise as big cats sneak up on their prey. When it is time to attack, the cats can flick out their claws to grip and slash. Lions and tigers also use their claws to climb trees.

It's amazing!

Lions and tigers often scratch trees to sharpen their claws, in the same way as pet cats scratch furniture!

How retractable claws work.

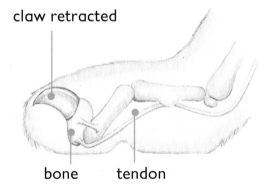

claw retracted

bone   tendon

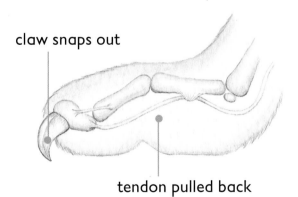

claw snaps out

tendon pulled back by leg muscle

9

Hunting

Lionesses are faster than male lions, so they do most of the hunting. These lionesses are chasing a gazelle.

Lions hunt gazelles, zebra and wildebeest. All these animals can run fast. Their speed, and the fact that the grasslands of Africa are very open, with few hiding places, make them hard to catch. Lions work together as a team. They surround their prey on different sides and then creep up on them. They choose the youngest and weakest animals in a group.

It's amazing!
Lions are the only cats that hunt together as a team.

Tigers are also fast and expert hunters. They hunt deer, pigs, buffalo and even baby elephants. If they are very hungry they will also eat monkeys and frogs. They will even lap up ants! Tigers hunt alone. They hunt at night – their eyesight is six times better than ours. They often wait by **waterholes** to **ambush** their prey.

Tigers are strong swimmers. They catch and eat fish and water birds, as well as land animals.

The kill!

When lions attack they try to trip or knock down their prey. They need to kill large and dangerous animals like buffalo quickly, without getting into a fight. They usually bite the throat, which breaks the neck or **suffocates** the animal very quickly. The males feed first, getting 'the lion's share'! Then the females and the cubs feed.

A lioness grabs a wildebeest by the throat.

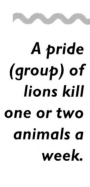

A pride (group) of lions kill one or two animals a week.

Tigers also leap on their prey and go for the throat. They drag their prey to a safer, hidden place to eat. Often the dead animal is too big for the tiger to eat all at once. They sometimes cover the body with earth and grass and come back to feed on it the next night.

It's amazing!
Only about one out of every twenty attacks that a tiger makes is successful.

Tigers often kill several animals a week.

Staying hidden

When lions creep up on their prey they need to stay hidden. A lioness' sandy yellow coat is good **camouflage** to keep her hidden against the dry grass, sun and shade. Male lions cannot hide as easily – their dark mane is easier to spot.

It's amazing!

Lion cubs have spots that make them hard to see in the low grass and bushes.

A lioness hides in the long grass.

Tigers seem too brightly coloured to hide, but in the jungles of India and Asia they are wonderfully camouflaged. A tiger's reddish-brown coat blends in with the leafy forests and grasslands, where the stripes look like the shadows of leaves and branches.

Indian tigers are hard to see in the open – and even harder to see in the long grass!

Family life

A family of lions is called a pride. Each pride has an area of land it hunts in, called its **territory**. A pride has about three or four males in it, with ten or more females and cubs. The strongest males defend the pride against attacks from hyenas and other male lions intruding on the territory. The lionesses do all the hunting. Most of the day male lions do nothing but lie in the shade and keep cool.

It's amazing!

Lions spend up to twenty hours a day resting!

A pride of lions.

Two tigers share a wild pig.

Tigers usually live alone, although some male and female tigers may live together for a while. Each tiger has a large hunting territory. A male tiger will sometimes share his territory with one or two females and even share his kill with them.

Defending territory

The strongest male lions lead the pride. Male cubs stay with the pride until they are about three years old, when the leaders drive them away. They live alone for two or three years, until they are big enough to try to join a pride by driving out one of the leaders. The males roar at each other until the weaker lion is driven away. Sometimes they fight.

Sometimes male lions who have left the pride hunt together. Few survive, as they are not as good at hunting as lionesses.

It's amazing!

If a new lion takes over a pride he will sometimes kill the old leader's cubs.

Male tigers defend their territory from other males. They will sometimes snarl and roar at other males to drive them away. When a tiger snarls it turns its ears down to show the white patches on the back of the ears. This is a warning sign! Sometimes tigers will also fight.

Two Bengal tigers fight in the water.

This Bengal tiger snarls and turns its ears down as a warning.

Cubs

When a female lion is about to have her cubs she leaves the pride and finds a safe place. She usually has two or three cubs. They are tiny and do not open their eyes for the first two weeks. Their mother guards them from other big cats and hyenas. After six weeks they all go back to live with the pride and the other lionesses help to feed and guard the cubs.

Cubs learn how to hunt and kill by playing and fighting.

It's amazing!

If a lioness dies the other females in the pride look after her cubs.

A lioness watches over her cubs.

Tigers also have two or three cubs. The mother keeps away from other tigers and hides her cubs when she goes out hunting. Male tigers will sometimes kill cubs, even their own. The cubs stay with their mother for about two years, learning how to hunt and kill by watching her.

A tigress carrying her cub by the scruff (loose fold of skin) at the back of the neck.

Fact file

Lion

~~~~~

Weight
A male lion
may weigh up
to 313 kg.

Lives in
Africa and
Northwest
India

Food
Zebra, antelope,
gazelle,
wildebeest,
giraffe, buffalo
and sometimes
smaller animals

Life span
15–20 years

Tiger

~~~~~~

Weight
A male Siberian (the largest tiger) can weigh up to 384 kg.

Lives in
India, Asia, Siberia

Food
Deer, pigs, buffalo, baby elephants, birds, fish and other smaller animals, even insects

Life span
15–20 years

Records
One male Siberian held in captivity grew to 3.32 m long and weighed 423 kg!

Glossary

ambush a surprise attack.

camouflage coloured or shaped in a way that makes an animal hard to see.

endangered species a group of living things whose numbers are so few that they may all die out and become extinct.

habitat the place in which an animal lives.

migrate to move from one area to another each year.

prey an animal that is hunted by another for food.

relations a very similar group of animals.

seasons parts of the year that have different weather (like summer and winter).

suffocate to stop another animal breathing.

territory an area that an animal defends against other animals of the same species.

waterhole a pond or part of a river where wild animals come to drink.

Index